Silly Joke Books

# SILLY JOKES ABOUT ANIMALS

by Michael Dahl

PEBBLE
a capstone imprint

Published by Pebble, an imprint of Capstone
1710 Roe Crest Drive, North Mankato, Minnesota 56003
capstonepub.com



Library of Congress Cataloging-in-Publication Data
Names: Dahl, Michael, author.
Title: Silly jokes about animals / by Michael Dahl.
Description: North Mankato, Minnesota : Pebble, [2022] | Series: Silly joke books | Audience: Ages: 5-8 | Audience: Grades: 2-3 | Summary: "Get ready to laugh from the farm to the pet store with these silly animal jokes! Hilarious images combined with laugh-out-loud jokes will have young readers clamoring for more"-- Provided by publisher.
Identifiers: LCCN 2021002850 (print) | LCCN 2021002851 (ebook) | ISBN 9781977131584 (hardcover) | ISBN 9781977154835 (pdf) | ISBN 9781977156495 (kindle edition)
Subjects: LCSH: Animals--Juvenile humor. | Wit and humor, Juvenile. Classification: LCC PN6231.A5 D38 2022 (print) | LCC PN6231.A5 (ebook) | DDC 808.88/2--dc23
LC record available at https://lccn.loc.gov/2021002850
LC ebook record available at https://lccn.loc.gov/2021002851

Editorial Credits
Editor: Christianne Jones; Designer: Brann Garvey and Mighty Media; Media Researcher: Jo Miller; Production Specialist: Laura Manthe

Image Credits
Shutterstock, 21, necklaces, ajt, 15, banana skin, ang intaravichian, 4, feather, antpkr, 18, squid, bennie, 18, squid, Billion Photos, 15, monkey, COZ, 19, Csanad Kiss, 5, dog, DenisNata, 8, duck, Entrieri, 21, hats, Eric Isselee, 14, lion, 17, leopard, Fesus Robert, 23, fotoslaz, 11, elephant, goldenjack, 16, guteksk7, 20, cell phones, heromen30, 6-7, money, innakreativ, 8, crackers, Jagodka, 9, JIANG HONGYAN, 15, banana skin, 18, squid, John Kasawa, 5, shorts, Mega Pixel, 12, glass slipper, nattawit.sree, 12, background, nevodka, 14, fork, pandapaw, 12, elephant, Petr Student, 18, bus, pets in frames, 3, 24, Photo Melon, 17, fan, picsbyst, Cover, 6, horse, Picsfive, 8, box, Rich Carey, 18, octopus, Robert Eastman, 8, duck, Romolo Tavani, 15, background, RTimages, 10, clock, schankz, 4, feather, souloff, design element, Spayder pauk_79, 20, oysters, stockphoto mania, 4, chicken, tanoochai, 21, fish, xmee, 5, gloves, yevgeniy11, 6, fence, 7, Zachary Hoover, 11, background



Printed in the United States 4687

# Table of Contents

# FARM FUNNIES

What side of a chicken has the most feathers?

**The outside.**

What do you call a sleeping bull?

**A bull-dozer.**

Why didn't the dog play football?

**It was a boxer.**

What happened to the horse when it swallowed a dollar bill?

**It bucked.**

Do you know why the pony was so quiet?

**Because it was a little hoarse.**

When does a horse talk?

**Whinny wants to.**

Why shouldn't you tell a secret to a pig?

**It will squeal.**

When do ducks wake up?

**At the quack of dawn.**

What do you call
a carton full of ducks?

**A box of quackers.**

Why was the cow afraid?

**He was a coward.**

What dog loves to take bubble baths?

**A shampoodle.**

# ELEPHANT LAUGHS

What should you do
if an elephant sneezes?

**Get out of its way!**

What time is it when an
elephant sits on your fence?

**Time to get a new fence.**

What time is it when 10
elephants are chasing you?

**Ten after one.**

CRACK!

IT FITS!

What weighs more than
4,000 pounds (1,814 kilograms)
and wears glass slippers?

**Cinderella-phant!**

What do you get when you
cross a fish with an elephant?

**Swimming trunks.**

What is very big, very blue,
and has a trunk?

**An elephant holding its
breath.**

# JUNGLE JOKERS

Why was the lion so happy after dinner?

**He enjoyed the mane course.**

How do you keep a rhino from charging?

**Take away its credit card.**

Why do monkeys like bananas?

**They have appeal.**

Why should you never play cards in the jungle?

**It's full of cheetahs.**

What fur do you get from a tiger?

**As fur as possible!**

Why are leopards so bad at
playing hide-and-seek?

**They're always spotted.**

# SEA SILLIES

How do squid get to work?

**They take the octo-bus.**

Why don't fish go on vacations?

**They're always in school.**

What day do fish hate?

**Fry-day.**

What are the strongest creatures in the ocean?

**Mussles.**

Why are fish bad at basketball?

**They're afraid of the net.**

How do oysters call each other?

**On shell phones.**

What do you call a fish that's dressed up in fancy clothes?

**So-fish-ticated.**

# ACTIVITY: ANIMAL ANTICS

**What you need:**

- paper
- scissors
- markers or crayons
- empty container

**What you do:**

1. Combine all your favorite animals into one. Cut sheets of paper into at least nine small pieces.
2. Write down a different animal on each piece of paper. Then put all the pieces into a container.
3. Pull out three pieces of paper from the bowl.
4. Look at the three animals you picked. Then make up a new animal that blends all three.
5. Draw a picture of the strange creature and give it a cool name.

# GLOSSARY

**appeal** (uh-PEEL)—something good that makes you like an object or person or animal

**mussle** (MUHS-uhl)—a type of shellfish that is found in saltwater and freshwater

**oyster** (OI-ster)—a shellfish that lives in shallow water

**whinny** (WIN-ee)—a type of sound a horse makes

# READ MORE

Dahl, Michael. *Scooby-Doo Animal Jokes. North Mankato*, MN: Capstone, 2015.

Pellowski, Michael J. *Mega-funny Jokes & Riddles.* New York: Sterling, 2017.

Winn, Whee. *Lots of Animal Jokes for Kids.* Grand Rapids, MI: Zonderkidz, 2020.

# INTERNET SITES

*Enchanted Learning*
www.enchantedlearning.com/jokes/topics/animal.shtml

*Funology*
www.funology.com/animal-jokes

# INDEX